jesus every day

Devotional Guide

CANDACE | DaySpring

candacecbure.com | dayspring.com

WELCOME!

I'm so glad you're joining me in this encouraging study on the topic of love!

The Bible is full of examples of how we can daily walk in love, and we'll explore these together. In this study, we'll learn from God's Word what it means to love, why we should love, and how we should love.

We are bombarded with so many different ideas about what love is, but what is it really? We're often told it's how we feel about someone or something, but God's definition is way different. Since *God* is love, *love begins with Him.* Without Him, we can't love ourselves, others, or even Him the way we should.

Colossians 3:14 reminds us that "over all" other virtues, we're to "put on love" (NIV). This means we need to allow love to drive everything about us—our kindness, selflessness, hope, joy, and more. None of us will ever be 100 percent perfect in the area of love, but if we are to shine a light in this dark world, *love over all* is what matters most.

In this together, *Candace*

Before You Get Started on This Adventure

$\mathcal{H}$ere's the deal. You're picking this book up and are either super excited to dig in or wondering if you really want to start this journey with me. I get it. Trust me, I do. And while I can tell you that this study can undoubtedly change your life, you may not be eager to jump in based on my enthusiasm alone. But would you do me a favor? Would you at least read through this first section before you put this book back on the shelf?

Before jumping into it, you might be wondering why the Bible is worth reading or what all the talk about being "saved" means. You may feel like you'll never measure up to God's standards—that there's no hope for you—so why even try? Or maybe you feel like you're doing just fine and life is actually pretty good, so why would you need to dig deep into God's Word?

Wherever you are in your spiritual journey, I want you to know you're not alone. In this first section, I've answered some questions people typically ask me about my Christian faith. I hope these answers will be helpful to you too.

Why should I read and study the Bible?

The world is full of all kinds of books that tell stories, teach concepts, inspire, and entertain. Heck, I've even written a few of them! Many books have influenced the world throughout history, but none compare with the Bible.

We all love a good story, right? While the Bible is full of history, wisdom, guidelines, and poetry, it's actually the epic story about all of creation and time from the beginning to the end. In the Bible, God is the ultimate storyteller—He shares His plan, His story, and His design for the world and for humanity.

The story begins with God creating His beloved humanity—Adam and Eve—in His image. But they destroyed their relationship with Him by choosing power instead of trusting in Him. Then the rest of the Bible—the greatest love story ever told—continues as God sets His plan in motion to bring His people back to Himself.

While there are other books that claim to be "holy," and even some that may contain useful ideas or wise words, no other book explains so clearly humanity's desperate need for rescue and how God Himself came to the rescue by sending His only Son, Jesus. No other book is so transformational because no other book shows us how much we are *loved* by our Creator.

What does it mean to be "saved"?

When followers of Jesus talk about being saved, we mean that Jesus rescued us from the ultimate consequence of sin—eternal separation from God—and our lives are no longer controlled by sin or filled with darkness, hopelessness, shame, guilt, and fear. Jesus shines His light, freedom, joy, peace, and hope into our lives. God doesn't want sin to have any control over us. He wants to have a relationship with us. He wants us to live full, abundant, joyful lives that reflect His goodness back to others! That's why Jesus came—to save us from the punishment we deserve because of our sin and to give us new life.

Being saved doesn't mean we are spared from all suffering in our lives. But it does mean we have God's presence with us and the promise of spending forever with Him—

an eternity free from all pain and suffering. Jesus is ready to save us the moment we open our hearts to Him and accept His unconditional love for us.

What if I don't need to be "saved"?

I get this too—you're a good person, you help others, you live honestly, you probably donate time and money to charity, and you're not hurting anyone. Why do you need to be "saved"? Compared to others, you're practically a saint! But God's standards are different from human standards. If we just compare ourselves to other people, it's easy to think we're good enough. But when we compare ourselves to God's standards, we fall miserably short. Every. Single. Time.

We all deserve God's judgment. Because He is holy, He cannot allow sin anywhere near Him. Because of sin, we cannot earn our way to having a relationship with God. Our sin separates us from our Creator. God says that if we break even one commandment, it's as if we're guilty of breaking them all. There isn't one of us who can say we are sinless. And doing good things to earn God's approval doesn't erase our sinfulness either. But because God loves us, He sent His Son, Jesus, to die so that all people—the bad, the good, and everyone in between—could have a relationship with Him.

$\mathcal{B}$ecause I believe the Bible shows us who Jesus is and how we can have a relationship with Him, I want to help you get to know Him too. That's what this study guide is all about.

How do I use this study guide?

Here's how it works: each day has a reading from the Bible and then some questions to help you think about and apply the biblical concepts. It's that simple! There's no "right" answer, and you can add your own questions and thoughts at any point, on any page.

Ideally, this is a personal journey where God will speak directly to your heart. But going through the study with friends can bring you encouragement and help you connect with others in really valuable ways. If you'd like, you could complete a day's study alone and then come together with a group of friends to discuss what God is showing you. You decide!

Let's do this!

As you go through each day's study, pray through it. Don't just complete it so you can check it off your to-do list. And don't look to me to tell you the answers or what to think; look to the Word and ask God to speak to you. Lastly, don't be afraid. The most repeated command in the Bible is "Do not fear," and one of the most common promises from God is "I am with you." So jump into this adventure and ask God what He wants to reveal to you.

Whether you are new to the Bible or super familiar with it, I can tell you this: God's Word is living and active. It will bring you life, and you will thrive every day as you find truth, peace, and hope within its pages. Let's go!

Love Is Patient

Ephesians 4:1–6; II Timothy 2:23–25 (CEV)

As a prisoner of the Lord, I beg you to live in a way that is worthy of the people God has chosen to be His own. Always be humble and gentle. Patiently put up with each other and love each other. Try your best to let God's Spirit keep your hearts united. Do this by living at peace. All of you are part of the same body. There is only one Spirit of God, just as you were given one hope when you were chosen to be God's people. We have only one Lord, one faith, and one baptism. There is one God who is the Father of all people. Not only is God above all others, but He works by using all of us, and He lives in all of us.

Stay away from stupid and senseless arguments. These only lead to trouble, and God's servants must not be troublemakers. They must be kind to everyone, and they must be good teachers and very patient.

Be humble when you correct people who oppose you. Maybe God will lead them to turn to Him and learn the truth.

When do you struggle most with being patient?

In these verses, what are the characteristics of someone who serves the Lord?

What can you learn from these verses about the connection between loving people and being patient? How can being patient with people help us avoid fighting and arguing?

WE REFLECT GOD'S CHARACTER WHEN WE'RE PATIENT WITH OTHERS.

Journal about a situation you're facing in which you need to demonstrate

love by being patient. Ask God to help you be lovingly patient.

A NOTE FROM CANDACE

Being a mom has stretched me. Every. Single. Day. My kids have grown me in ways I never knew possible. It's challenging to love day in, day out. Especially when we're not all agreeable.

But the patience I've received from God and the love I get from my children is heaven sent.

DAY 2

Love
Is Kind

RUTH 2:2–12 (NLT)

One day Ruth the Moabite said to Naomi, "Let me go out into the harvest fields to pick up the stalks of grain left behind by anyone who is kind enough to let me do it."

Naomi replied, "All right, my daughter, go ahead." So Ruth went out to gather grain behind the harvesters. And as it happened, she found herself working in a field that belonged to Boaz, the relative of her father-in-law, Elimelech. . . .

Boaz went over and said to Ruth, "Listen, my daughter. Stay right here with us when you gather grain; don't go to any other fields. Stay right behind the young women working in my field. See which part of the field they are harvesting, and then follow them. I have warned the young men not to treat you roughly. And when you are thirsty, help yourself to the water they have drawn from the well."

Ruth fell at his feet and thanked him warmly. "What have I done to deserve such kindness?" she asked. "I am only a foreigner."

"Yes, I know," Boaz replied. "But I also know about everything you have done for your mother-in-law since the death of your husband. I have heard how you left your father and mother and your own land to live here among complete strangers. May the LORD, the God of Israel, under whose wings you have come to take refuge, reward you fully for what you have done."

Describe a time when you showed kindness to a stranger. What happened?

How did Ruth demonstrate her love for Naomi in this story?

In what ways did Boaz show kindness to Ruth?

KINDNESS

IS LOVE IN

ACTION.

How has God showered His kindness on you? Who is someone in

your life who could use that same measure of kindness?

YOUR BIGGEST TAKEAWAY

Love Is Humble

JOHN 13:3–15 (CSB)

Jesus knew that the Father had given everything into His hands, that He had come from God, and that He was going back to God. So He got up from supper, laid aside His outer clothing, took a towel, and tied it around Himself. Next, He poured water into a basin and began to wash His disciples' feet and to dry them with the towel tied around Him.

He came to Simon Peter, who asked Him, "Lord, are You going to wash my feet?" . . .

"One who has bathed," Jesus told him, "doesn't need to wash anything except his feet, but he is completely clean. You are clean, but not all of you." For He knew who would betray Him. This is why He said, "Not all of you are clean."

When Jesus had washed their feet and put on His outer clothing, He reclined again and said to them, "Do you know what I have done for you? You call Me Teacher and Lord—and you are speaking rightly, since that is what I am. So if I, your Lord and Teacher, have washed your feet, you also ought to wash one another's feet. For I have given you an example, that you also should do just as I have done for you."

Who is the humblest person you know? What makes him or her so humble?

What physical actions did Jesus do to demonstrate humility?

Why do you think Jesus took the posture of a servant and washed His disciples' feet?

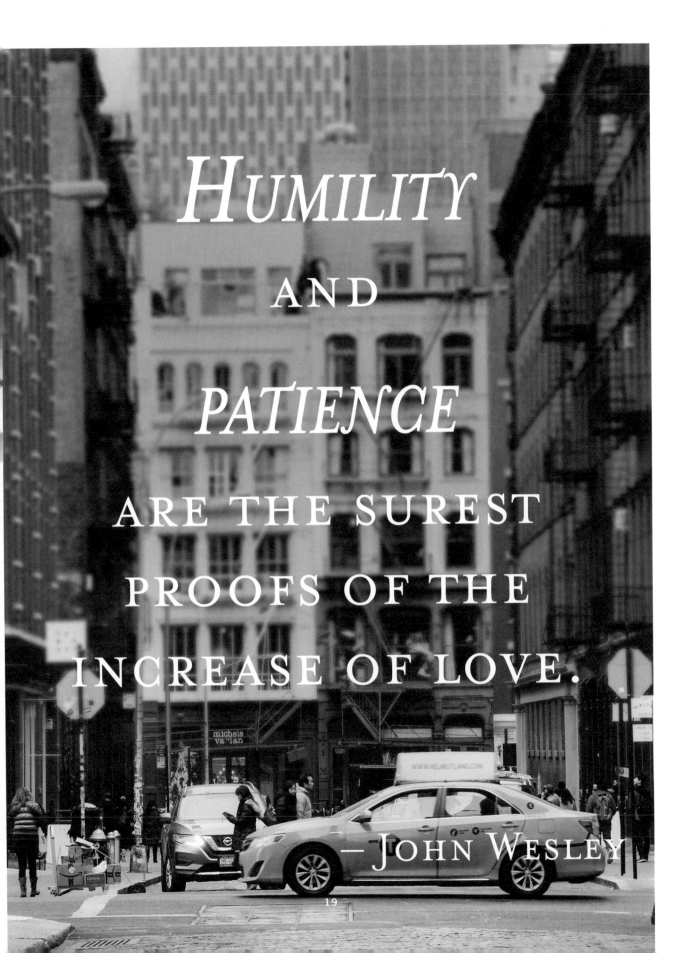

HUMILITY AND PATIENCE ARE THE SUREST PROOFS OF THE INCREASE OF LOVE.

— JOHN WESLEY

19

What is one practical action you can take this week to humbly serve someone?

YOUR BIGGEST TAKEAWAY

Love
Is Selfless

21

Hebrews 13:1–5, 7–8, 15–16 (NIV)

Keep on loving one another as brothers and sisters. Do not forget to show hospitality to strangers, for by so doing some people have shown hospitality to angels without knowing it. Continue to remember those in prison as if you were together with them in prison, and those who are mistreated as if you yourselves were suffering.

Marriage should be honored by all, and the marriage bed kept pure, for God will judge the adulterer and all the sexually immoral. Keep your lives free from the love of money and be content with what you have, because God has said,

> "Never will I leave you;
> never will I forsake you." . . .

Remember your leaders, who spoke the word of God to you. Consider the outcome of their way of life and imitate their faith. Jesus Christ is the same yesterday and today and forever. . . .

Through Jesus, therefore, let us continually offer to God a sacrifice of praise—the fruit of lips that openly profess His name. And do not forget to do good and to share with others, for with such sacrifices God is pleased.

When you hear the word **sacrifice** *or* **selfless,** *who or what comes to mind?*

Based on these verses, what kinds of sacrifices—acts of selflessness—please God?

Jesus offered His life as the ultimate sacrifice because of His love for us. What sacrifices are you willing to make for people to show your love for them?

ONLY GOD

CAN GIVE US A SELFLESS LOVE FOR OTHERS, AS THE

HOLY SPIRIT

CHANGES US WITHIN.

— BILLY GRAHAM

How do the words in these verses inspire you to love others and live more selflessly?

_____

_____

_____

_____

_____

_____

_____

_____

_____

_____

_____

_____

_____

_____

_____

_____

A NOTE FROM CANDACE

Marriage is no walk in the park. It takes *work*! Our marriage is grounded in God's Word. He is the center of our marriage—the foundation and blueprint for how we live. Successful relationships involve being open and honest and ultimately doing what pleases God, not living selfishly.

Love Is Forgiving

GENESIS 37:23–24, 28; 50:15–21 (ESV)

When Joseph came to his brothers, they stripped him of his robe, the robe of many colors that he wore. And they took him and threw him into a pit. The pit was empty; there was no water in it. . . . Then Midianite traders passed by. And [Joseph's brothers] drew Joseph up and lifted him out of the pit, and sold him to the Ishmaelites for twenty shekels of silver. They took Joseph to Egypt. . . .

[Many years later,] when Joseph's brothers saw that their father was dead, they said, "It may be that Joseph will hate us and pay us back for all the evil that we did to him." So they sent a message to Joseph, saying, "Your father gave this command before he died: 'Say to Joseph, "Please forgive the transgression of your brothers and their sin, because they did evil to you."' And now, please forgive the transgression of the servants of the God of your father." Joseph wept when they spoke to him. His brothers also came and fell down before him and said, "Behold, we are your servants." But Joseph said to them, "Do not fear, for am I in the place of God? As for you, you meant evil against me, but God meant it for good, to bring it about that many people should be kept alive, as they are today. So do not fear; I will provide for you and your little ones." Thus he comforted them and spoke kindly to them.

*For more on Joseph's story, read Genesis 37; 39–50.

When have you struggled to forgive someone?

How did Joseph, who was sold into slavery by his own

brothers, demonstrate genuine forgiveness?

How does this story inspire or challenge you?

FORGIVENESS IS THE HIGHEST FORM OF *LOVE.*

Use this space to write a prayer to God, thanking Him for His forgiveness and asking for His help to genuinely forgive someone who's wronged you.

YOUR BIGGEST TAKEAWAY

Love
Is Active
and Truthful

I JOHN 3:16–24 (NIV)

This is how we know what love is: Jesus Christ laid down His life for us. And we ought to lay down our lives for our brothers and sisters. If anyone has material possessions and sees a brother or sister in need but has no pity on them, how can the love of God be in that person? Dear children, let us not love with words or speech but with actions and in truth.

This is how we know that we belong to the truth and how we set our hearts at rest in His presence: If our hearts condemn us, we know that God is greater than our hearts, and He knows everything. Dear friends, if our hearts do not condemn us, we have confidence before God and receive from Him anything we ask, because we keep His commands and do what pleases Him. And this is His command: to believe in the name of His Son, Jesus Christ, and to love one another as He commanded us. The one who keeps God's commands lives in Him, and He in them. And this is how we know that He lives in us: We know it by the Spirit He gave us.

How would you define love based on these verses?

How do these verses urge us to show the truth of our love instead of just saying we love someone?

Why do you think actions are so much more powerful than words? How do our loving actions demonstrate that we "belong to the truth"?

WE WILL SPEAK THE *TRUTH IN LOVE,* GROWING IN EVERY WAY MORE AND MORE LIKE *CHRIST.*

— EPHESIANS 4:15 (NLT)

In what ways does the truth about Jesus and what He has done

for you compel you to actively love other people?

YOUR BIGGEST TAKEAWAY

Love Is Hopeful

Psalm 33:13–22 (CSB)

|

The LORD looks down from heaven;

He observes everyone.

He gazes on all the inhabitants of the earth

from His dwelling place.

He forms the hearts of them all;

He considers all their works.

A king is not saved by a large army;

a warrior will not be rescued by great strength.

The horse is a false hope for safety;

it provides no escape by its great power.

But look, the LORD keeps His eye on those who fear Him—

those who depend on His faithful love

to rescue them from death

and to keep them alive in famine.

We wait for the LORD;

He is our help and shield.

For our hearts rejoice in Him

because we trust in His holy name.

May Your faithful love rest on us, LORD,

for we put our hope in You.

What reasons do you have to trust in God and hope in His promises?

What are some of the reasons the psalmist gives in these verses for why we can place our hope in God?

Why might things of this world—such as strong armies and human strength— provide us with "false hope"? Why can we hope in God instead?

LOVE
ALWAYS HOPES FOR
THE BEST.

We often misplace our hope in people or situations. In what ways do you

need to change your focus and place your hope only in God?

A NOTE FROM CANDACE

It can be so easy to place our hope for meaningful relationships, successful careers, and healthy lives in all the great things we do and the strong people who support us. But the things we do and the support we receive ultimately can't measure up to the God who loves us and promises to help us. He will never let us down.

DAY 8

Love
Is Enduring

Deuteronomy 7:7–9, 12–15 (NIV)

The LORD did not set His affection on you [Israel] and choose you because you were more numerous than other peoples, for you were the fewest of all peoples. But it was because the LORD loved you and kept the oath He swore to your ancestors that He brought you out with a mighty hand and redeemed you from the land of slavery, from the power of Pharaoh king of Egypt. Know therefore that the LORD your God is God; He is the faithful God, keeping His covenant of love to a thousand generations of those who love Him and keep His commandments. . . .

If you pay attention to these laws and are careful to follow them, then the LORD your God will keep His covenant of love with you, as He swore to your ancestors. He will love you and bless you and increase your numbers. He will bless the fruit of your womb, the crops of your land—your grain, new wine and olive oil—the calves of your herds and the lambs of your flocks in the land He swore to your ancestors to give you. You will be blessed more than any other people; none of your men or women will be childless, nor will any of your livestock be without young. The LORD will keep you free from every disease. He will not inflict on you the horrible diseases you knew in Egypt, but He will inflict them on all who hate you.

How would you describe the difference between God's love and human love?

According to these verses, how had God shown His love to the people of Israel? How would He continue to show them His love?

What can you learn from these verses about God's love for His people— all who "love Him and keep His commandments"?

THREE THINGS WILL LAST FOREVER—

FAITH, HOPE, AND LOVE

—AND THE GREATEST OF THESE IS LOVE.

— I CORINTHIANS 13:13 (NLT)

In Malachi 3:6 Gods says, "I the LORD do not change" (NIV). Consider God's love for the people of Israel and His unchanging nature. How does this help you better understand His enduring love for you?

YOUR BIGGEST TAKEAWAY

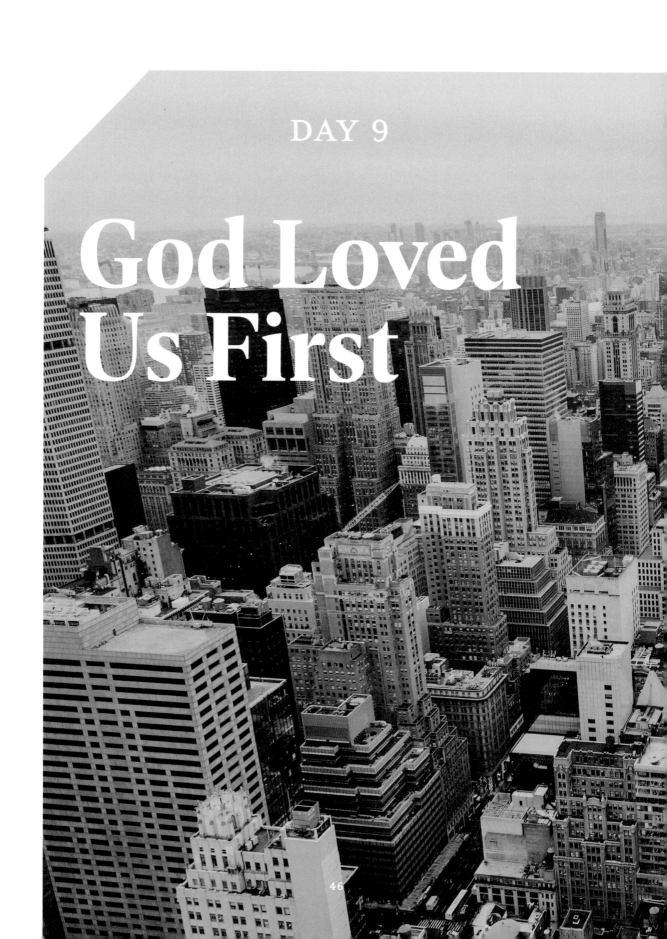

DAY 9

God Loved Us First

I John 4:13–21 (CEV)

God has given us His Spirit. That is how we know that we are one with Him, just as He is one with us. God sent His Son to be the Savior of the world. We saw His Son and are now telling others about Him. God stays one with everyone who openly says that Jesus is the Son of God. That's how we stay one with God and are sure that God loves us.

God is love. If we keep on loving others, we will stay one in our hearts with God, and He will stay one with us. If we truly love others and live as Christ did in this world, we won't be worried about the day of judgment. A real love for others will chase those worries away. The thought of being punished is what makes us afraid. It shows that we have not really learned to love.

We love because God loved us first. But if we say we love God and don't love each other, we are liars. We cannot see God. So how can we love God, if we don't love the people we can see? The commandment that God has given us is: "Love God and love each other!"

How do you know God loves you? In what ways do you doubt His love for you?

What is the definition of love based on these verses?

Why do you think it's inconceivable to say you love God
while at the same time you don't love people?

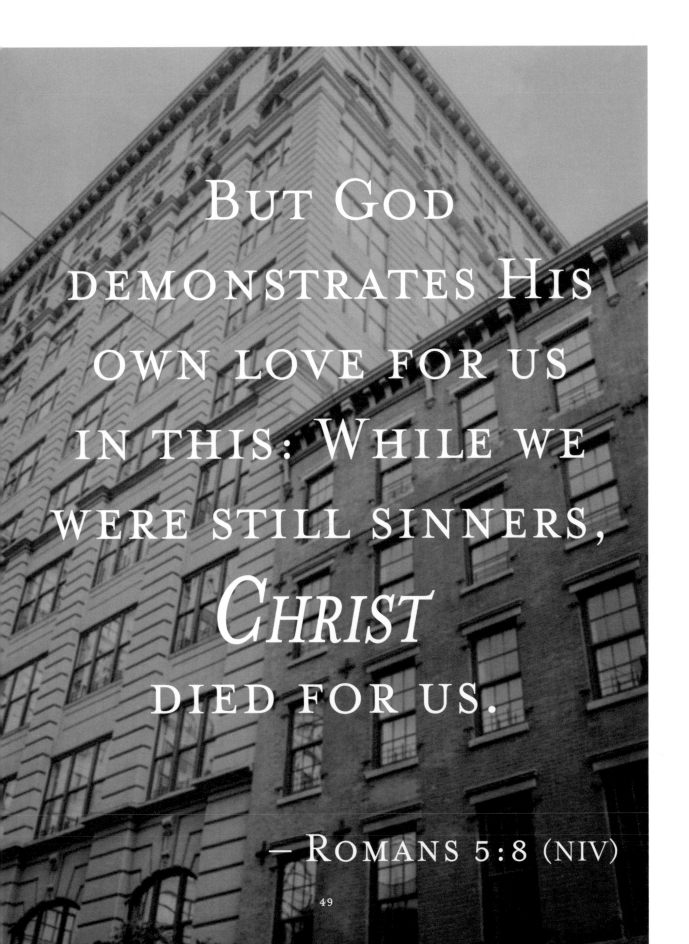

But God demonstrates His own love for us in this: While we were still sinners, *Christ* died for us.

— Romans 5:8 (NIV)

Use this space to write a love letter to God. Be sure to thank Him for specific

ways that He has shown you love. Tell Him why you love Him.

YOUR BIGGEST TAKEAWAY

Children of God

Matthew 5:38—48 (NIV)

"You have heard that it was said, 'Eye for eye, and tooth for tooth.' But I tell you, do not resist an evil person. If anyone slaps you on the right cheek, turn to them the other cheek also. And if anyone wants to sue you and take your shirt, hand over your coat as well. If anyone forces you to go one mile, go with them two miles. Give to the one who asks you, and do not turn away from the one who wants to borrow from you.

"You have heard that it was said, 'Love your neighbor and hate your enemy.' But I tell you, love your enemies and pray for those who persecute you, that you may be children of your Father in heaven. He causes His sun to rise on the evil and the good, and sends rain on the righteous and the unrighteous. If you love those who love you, what reward will you get? Are not even the tax collectors doing that? And if you greet only your own people, what are you doing more than others? Do not even pagans do that? Be perfect, therefore, as your heavenly Father is perfect."

Why do you think it's important for God's children to show love?

How does this passage surprise or challenge you?

According to these verses, in what ways should children of God—those who place their trust in God's Son, Jesus—show love to people?

NOTHING YOU DO IN THIS LIFE WILL EVER MATTER UNLESS IT'S ABOUT LOVING *GOD* AND LOVING THE PEOPLE *HE HAS MADE.*

— FRANCIS CHAN

How specifically do you need to love more like God loves? Ask God to help you

love like Him, and record some practical ways you can do this today.

_____

_____

_____

_____

_____

_____

_____

_____

_____

_____

_____

_____

_____

_____

_____

A NOTE FROM CANDACE

As a child of God, I need to reflect the love of my Father and represent Him accurately. That means I love and respect the person who disagrees with my beliefs, my choices, or even my political views. It's not easy, but it's the only way to live as a child of God.

No Greater Love

JOHN 13:31–35; 15:9–13 (NLT)

Jesus said [to His disciples], "The time has come for the Son of Man to enter into His glory, and God will be glorified because of Him. And since God receives glory because of the Son, He will give His own glory to the Son, and He will do so at once. Dear children, I will be with you only a little longer. And as I told the Jewish leaders, you will search for Me, but you can't come where I am going. So now I am giving you a new commandment: Love each other. Just as I have loved you, you should love each other. Your love for one another will prove to the world that you are My disciples. . . .

"I have loved you even as the Father has loved Me. Remain in My love. When you obey My commandments, you remain in My love, just as I obey My Father's commandments and remain in His love. I have told you these things so that you will be filled with My joy. Yes, your joy will overflow! This is My commandment: Love each other in the same way I have loved you. There is no greater love than to lay down one's life for one's friends."

Do you think how you love others points people to Jesus? Why or why not?

According to these verses, how can we "remain" in the love of Jesus?

What do you think Jesus meant by saying, "There is no greater love than to lay down one's life for one's friends"?

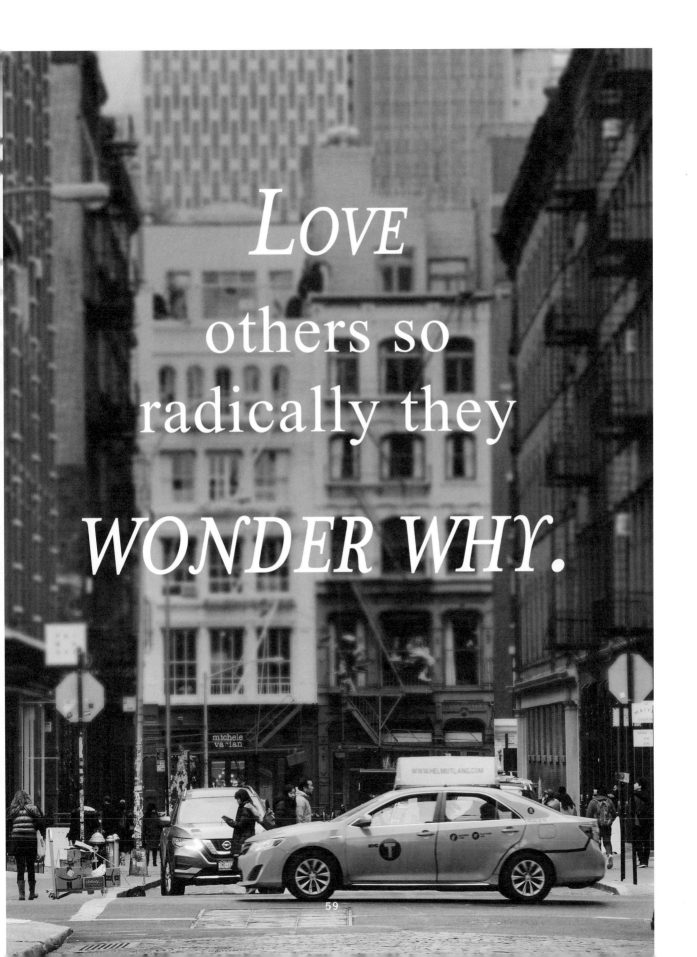

LOVE others so radically they *WONDER WHY.*

What are some practical ways you can lay your life down for others this week? In
which areas of your life do you need to love others the way Jesus loves you?

_____

_____

_____

_____

_____

_____

_____

_____

_____

_____

_____

_____

_____

YOUR BIGGEST TAKEAWAY

Love
Trusts

Psalm 32:5–11 (NLT)

Finally, I confessed all my sins to You
and stopped trying to hide my guilt.
I said to myself, "I will confess my rebellion to the LORD."
And You forgave me! All my guilt is gone. *Interlude*

Therefore, let all the godly pray to You while there is still time,
that they may not drown in the floodwaters of judgment.
For You are my hiding place;
You protect me from trouble.
You surround me with songs of victory. *Interlude*

The LORD says, "I will guide you along the best pathway for your life.
I will advise you and watch over you.
Do not be like a senseless horse or mule
that needs a bit and bridle to keep it under control."

Many sorrows come to the wicked,
but unfailing love surrounds those who trust the LORD.
So rejoice in the LORD and be glad, all you who obey Him!
Shout for joy, all you whose hearts are pure!

What are the qualities of a trustworthy person?

In these verses from Psalm 32, what are the reasons the author (David) gives for trusting God?

Based on these verses, what are the benefits of trusting God? How should those who trust God respond to His love for them?

UNFAILING *LOVE* SURROUNDS THOSE WHO TRUST THE *LORD.*

In what areas of your life are you still struggling to trust God? If you'd like, write a prayer, asking God to help you completely trust Him, obey Him, and accept His unfailing love for you.

YOUR BIGGEST TAKEAWAY

DAY 13

Love
Serves

ROMANS 13:8–10; GALATIANS 5:13–15 (CEV)

Let love be your only debt! If you love others, you have done all that the Law demands. In the Law there are many commands, such as, "Be faithful in marriage. Do not murder. Do not steal. Do not want what belongs to others." But all of these are summed up in the command that says, "Love others as much as you love yourself." No one who loves others will harm them. So love is all that the Law demands.

My friends, you were chosen to be free. So don't use your freedom as an excuse to do anything you want. Use it as an opportunity to serve each other with love. All that the Law says can be summed up in the command to love others as much as you love yourself. But if you keep attacking each other like wild animals, you had better watch out or you will destroy yourselves.

How much do you love and serve yourself compared to

how much you love and serve other people?

"Let love be your only debt!" How do these words change

your perspective on loving other people?

Trusting in Jesus for salvation brings us freedom from the consequences of our

sin. According to these verses, how should we respond to that freedom?

Serve each other with *LOVE.*

What are some specific ways you can serve others with love today?

A NOTE FROM CANDACE

We might be tempted to list all the good things we should do, cross each good thing off that list when we've completed it, and then give ourselves a pat on the back. But serving others isn't a to-do list. Love for people is a constant flowing spring within us that should just keep bubbling over. And Jesus is the source of that love.

DAY 14

Love Conquers Fear

Romans 8:28, 31–39 (NIV)

And we know that in all things God works for the good of those who love Him, who have been called according to His purpose. . . .

What, then, shall we say in response to these things? If God is for us, who can be against us? He who did not spare His own Son, but gave Him up for us all—how will He not also, along with Him, graciously give us all things? Who will bring any charge against those whom God has chosen? It is God who justifies. Who then is the one who condemns? No one. Christ Jesus who died—more than that, who was raised to life—is at the right hand of God and is also interceding for us. Who shall separate us from the love of Christ? Shall trouble or hardship or persecution or famine or nakedness or danger or sword? As it is written:

"For Your sake we face death all day long;
we are considered as sheep to be slaughtered."

No, in all these things we are more than conquerors through Him who loved us. For I am convinced that neither death nor life, neither angels nor demons, neither the present nor the future, nor any powers, neither height nor depth, nor anything else in all creation, will be able to separate us from the love of God that is in Christ Jesus our Lord.

Have you ever looked back on what seemed like a hopeless or difficult situation and realized there was good that came from it? What did you learn from that experience?

The first part of today's reading says, "In all things God works for the good of those who love Him." How do these words encourage you today?

The Bible promises us that nothing—including sickness, heartbreak, depression, loneliness, and fear—can separate us from God's love. How can this promise from the Bible help you when you face fearful situations ahead?

WE ARE MORE THAN *CONQUERORS* THROUGH HIM WHO *LOVED US.*

What situations in your life are causing you to fear or to doubt God's love for you? Write those down. If you'd like, write a prayer, thanking God for His promise to work things out for your good and for loving you through every situation. Ask Him to encourage you through the promises in the Bible.

YOUR BIGGEST TAKEAWAY

Love Glorifies God

PSALM 86:5–13 (NIV)

You, Lord, are forgiving and good,
  abounding in love to all who call to You.
Hear my prayer, LORD;
  listen to my cry for mercy.
When I am in distress, I call to You,
  because You answer me.

Among the gods there is none like You, Lord;
  no deeds can compare with Yours.
All the nations You have made
  will come and worship before You, Lord;
  they will bring glory to Your name.
For You are great and do marvelous deeds;
  You alone are God.

Teach me Your way, LORD,
  that I may rely on Your faithfulness;
give me an undivided heart,
  that I may fear Your name.
I will praise You, Lord my God, with all my heart;
  I will glorify Your name forever.
For great is Your love toward me.

What do you think it means to glorify God?

Name some of the attributes and actions King David (the writer of Psalm 86) recalls that demonstrate God's love. Which of these attributes can you most relate to?

Why do you think the psalmist is compelled to praise God's name forever?

LET ALL THAT YOU DO BE DONE WITH *LOVE.*

— I CORINTHIANS 16:14 (NKJV)

How can you bring glory to God by loving others? Ask God to show you specific ways to accomplish this. Then do it!

_____
_____
_____
_____
_____
_____
_____
_____
_____
_____
_____
_____
_____
_____

YOUR BIGGEST TAKEAWAY

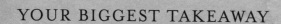

Love Shines in the Darkness

JOHN 1:9; 3:16–21; 12:46 (NLT)

The One who is the true light, who gives light to everyone, was coming into the world.

"For this is how God loved the world: He gave His one and only Son, so that everyone who believes in Him will not perish but have eternal life. God sent His Son into the world not to judge the world, but to save the world through Him.

"There is no judgment against anyone who believes in Him. But anyone who does not believe in Him has already been judged for not believing in God's one and only Son. And the judgment is based on this fact: God's light came into the world, but people loved the darkness more than the light, for their actions were evil. All who do evil hate the light and refuse to go near it for fear their sins will be exposed. But those who do what is right come to the light so others can see that they are doing what God wants."

"I have come as a light to shine in this dark world, so that all who put their trust in Me will no longer remain in the dark."

In what ways could light be compared with love?

In what ways could darkness be compared with evil?

According to these verses, how did God show His love to the world?

How did people respond to God's love?

Why do you think some people accept God's light but others reject it?

IF WE LOVE *OTHERS,* WE ARE IN THE *LIGHT.*

— I JOHN 2:10 (CEV)

Use this space to journal about your response to God's immense love for you. If you'd like, write a prayer, asking God to help you shine the light of His love in the darkness around you.

A NOTE FROM CANDACE

This world can be dark and ugly and sinful and evil. But Jesus has already brought us light. It's up to you and me—those of us who follow Jesus—to find every opportunity to let our lights shine so more and more people can walk into the light of God's love.

Loving Jesus

LUKE 7:36–47 (NIV)

When one of the Pharisees invited Jesus to have dinner with him, He went to the Pharisee's house and reclined at the table. A woman in that town who lived a sinful life learned that Jesus was eating at the Pharisee's house, so she came there with an alabaster jar of perfume. As she stood behind Him at His feet weeping, she began to wet His feet with her tears. Then she wiped them with her hair, kissed them and poured perfume on them.

When the Pharisee who had invited Him saw this, he said to himself, "If this man were a prophet, He would know who is touching Him and what kind of woman she is—that she is a sinner." . . .

Then [Jesus] turned toward the woman and said to Simon, "Do you see this woman? I came into your house. You did not give Me any water for My feet, but she wet My feet with her tears and wiped them with her hair. You did not give Me a kiss, but this woman, from the time I entered, has not stopped kissing My feet. You did not put oil on My head, but she has poured perfume on My feet. Therefore, I tell you, her many sins have been forgiven—as her great love has shown. But whoever has been forgiven little loves little."

What is the most extravagant display of love you've ever seen? Explain.

In what ways did the sinful woman show her love to Jesus? How did other people respond to her display of love? How did Jesus respond?

Why do you think the woman displayed her love for Jesus so extravagantly? What do you think Jesus meant when He said, "Whoever has been forgiven little loves little"?

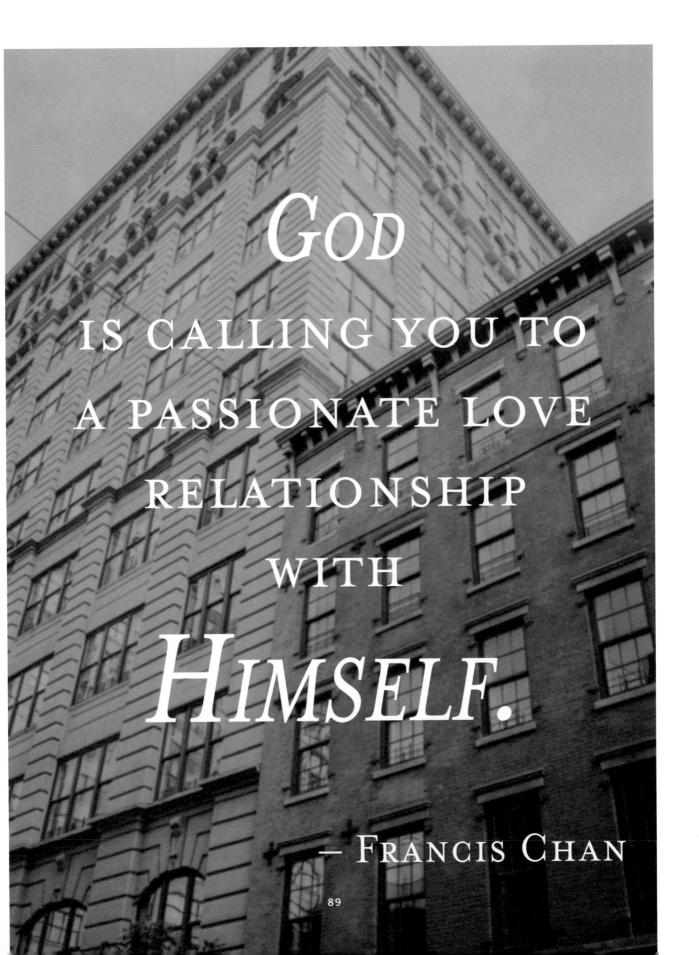

GOD
IS CALLING YOU TO
A PASSIONATE LOVE
RELATIONSHIP
WITH
HIMSELF.

— FRANCIS CHAN

Take a few moments to ask Jesus how you can love Him better—even extravagantly. Journal your thoughts and prayer here.

YOUR BIGGEST TAKEAWAY

Giving Generously

Philippians 4:10—19 (NLT)

How I [Paul] praise the Lord that you are concerned about me again. I know you have always been concerned for me, but you didn't have the chance to help me. Not that I was ever in need, for I have learned how to be content with whatever I have. I know how to live on almost nothing or with everything. I have learned the secret of living in every situation, whether it is with a full stomach or empty, with plenty or little. For I can do everything through Christ, who gives me strength. Even so, you have done well to share with me in my present difficulty.

As you know, you Philippians were the only ones who gave me financial help when I first brought you the Good News and then traveled on from Macedonia. No other church did this. Even when I was in Thessalonica you sent help more than once. I don't say this because I want a gift from you. Rather, I want you to receive a reward for your kindness.

At the moment I have all I need—and more! I am generously supplied with the gifts you sent me with Epaphroditus. They are a sweet-smelling sacrifice that is acceptable and pleasing to God. And this same God who takes care of me will supply all your needs from His glorious riches, which have been given to us in Christ Jesus.

Describe a time when you benefited from someone's generosity. How did this situation affect you?

Paul wrote these verses as part of a letter to Christians in the city of Philippi.

In what ways had the recipients of Paul's letter generously cared for Paul?

What does this passage reveal about how God views our generosity?

LOVE
ALWAYS COSTS US
SOMETHING.

Consider people and organizations that could benefit from your time, resources, and talents. How can you demonstrate God's love through generosity?

YOUR BIGGEST TAKEAWAY

Treating People with Gentleness

I Thessalonians 2:4–12 (CSB)

Just as we have been approved by God to be entrusted with the gospel, so we speak, not to please people, but rather God, who examines our hearts. For we never used flattering speech, as you know, or had greedy motives—God is our witness—and we didn't seek glory from people, either from you or from others. Although we could have been a burden as Christ's apostles, instead we were gentle among you, as a nurse nurtures her own children. We cared so much for you that we were pleased to share with you not only the gospel of God but also our own lives, because you had become dear to us. For you remember our labor and hardship, brothers and sisters. Working night and day so that we would not burden any of you, we preached God's gospel to you. You are witnesses, and so is God, of how devoutly, righteously, and blamelessly we conducted ourselves with you believers. As you know, like a father with his own children, we encouraged, comforted, and implored each one of you to live worthy of God, who calls you into His own kingdom and glory.

How do you tend to respond to people who harshly criticize you for your beliefs?

In his letter, the apostle Paul explained how he and his companions treated the Christians in the city of Thessalonica. In what ways did Paul treat people with gentleness rather than harshness?

How do "flattering speech," "greedy motives," and seeking "glory from people" weaken our ability to treat people with love and gentleness?

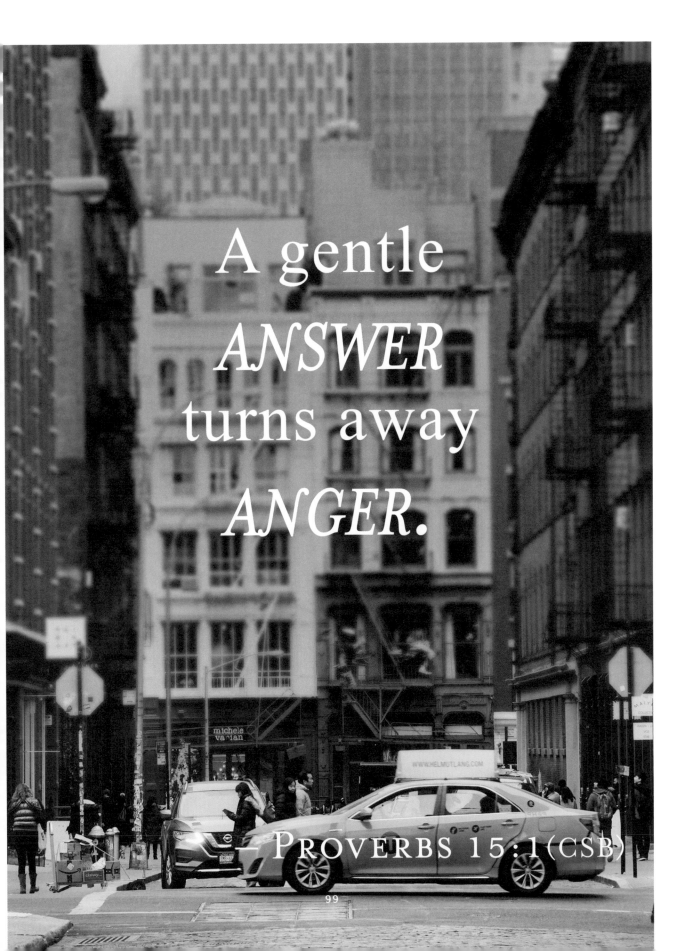

A gentle *ANSWER* turns away *ANGER.*

— Proverbs 15:1 (CSB)

In what ways are your actions and speech habits lacking in gentleness? How can

you more effectively love people through gentle words and responses?

A NOTE FROM CANDACE

Treating people with gentleness doesn't mean we need to be passive and weak. It means we treat those who oppose us or dislike us with respect. Look at Jesus. He's the ultimate example of someone who chose to respond with love, gentleness, and respect to those who were mocking Him and about to kill Him.

Showing Mercy

JOHN 8:2—11 (ESV)

Early in the morning [Jesus] came again to the temple. All the people came to him, and he sat down and taught them. The scribes and the Pharisees brought a woman who had been caught in adultery, and placing her in the midst they said to him, "Teacher, this woman has been caught in the act of adultery. Now in the Law, Moses commanded us to stone such women. So what do you say?" This they said to test him, that they might have some charge to bring against him. Jesus bent down and wrote with his finger on the ground. And as they continued to ask him, he stood up and said to them, "Let him who is without sin among you be the first to throw a stone at her." And once more he bent down and wrote on the ground. But when they heard it, they went away one by one, beginning with the older ones, and Jesus was left alone with the woman standing before him. Jesus stood up and said to her, "Woman, where are they? Has no one condemned you?" She said, "No one, Lord." And Jesus said, "Neither do I condemn you; go, and from now on sin no more."

In what ways do you show mercy to people on a daily basis? In what ways do you find it difficult to show mercy?

How did Jesus lovingly show mercy to the accused woman? How did she respond to Him?

What can you learn about Jesus' love and His mercy from this passage?

What does the Lord require *OF YOU?* To act justly and to love *MERCY* and to walk humbly with your *GOD.*

— MICAH 6:8 (NIV)

How can you be more like Jesus by showing mercy to those around you?

Journal about some practical ways you can show love by being merciful.

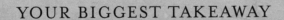

YOUR BIGGEST TAKEAWAY

Obeying God

JOHN 14:15—21; I JOHN 5:1—5 (NIV)

"If you love Me [Jesus], keep My commands. And I will ask the Father, and He will give you another advocate to help you and be with you forever—the Spirit of truth. The world cannot accept Him, because it neither sees Him nor knows Him. But you know Him, for He lives with you and will be in you. I will not leave you as orphans; I will come to you. Before long, the world will not see Me anymore, but you will see Me. Because I live, you also will live. On that day you will realize that I am in My Father, and you are in Me, and I am in you. Whoever has My commands and keeps them is the one who loves Me. The one who loves Me will be loved by My Father, and I too will love them and show Myself to them."

Everyone who believes that Jesus is the Christ is born of God, and everyone who loves the father loves his child as well. This is how we know that we love the children of God: by loving God and carrying out His commands. In fact, this is love for God: to keep His commands. And His commands are not burdensome, for everyone born of God overcomes the world. This is the victory that has overcome the world, even our faith. Who is it that overcomes the world? Only the one who believes that Jesus is the Son of God.

What does our obedience to God say about our love for Him?

What do these verses reveal about the connection between love and obedience?

According to these verses, what attitudes and actions please God?

What attitudes and actions should we avoid?

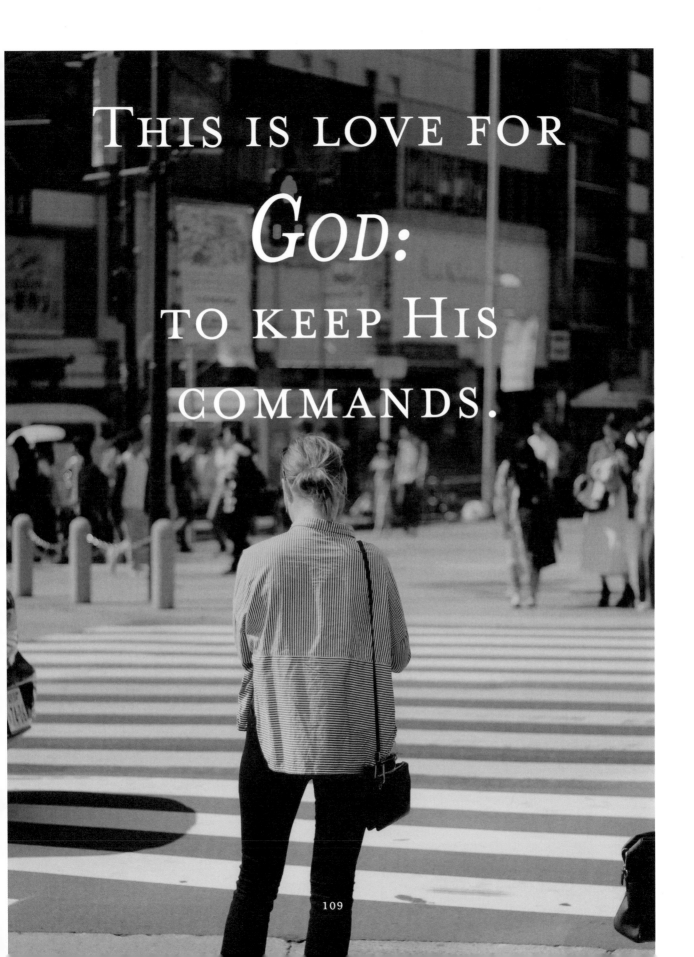

THIS IS LOVE FOR *GOD*: TO KEEP HIS COMMANDS.

How did this passage challenge or encourage you? If you'd like, write

a prayer, asking God to help you obey Him more completely.

YOUR BIGGEST TAKEAWAY

Responding to Human Need

LUKE 10:25–37 (ESV)

And behold, a lawyer stood up to put [Jesus] to the test, saying, "Teacher, what shall I do to inherit eternal life?" He said to him, "What is written in the Law? How do you read it?" And he answered, "You shall love the Lord your God with all your heart and with all your soul and with all your strength and with all your mind, and your neighbor as yourself." And he said to him, "You have answered correctly; do this, and you will live."

But he, desiring to justify himself, said to Jesus, "And who is my neighbor?" Jesus replied, "A man was going down from Jerusalem to Jericho, and he fell among robbers, who stripped him and beat him and departed, leaving him half dead. Now by chance a priest was going down that road, and when he saw him he passed by on the other side. So likewise a Levite, when he came to the place and saw him, passed by on the other side. But a Samaritan, as he journeyed, came to where he was, and when he saw him, he had compassion. He went to him and bound up his wounds, pouring on oil and wine. Then he set him on his own animal and brought him to an inn and took care of him. And the next day he took out two denarii and gave them to the innkeeper, saying, 'Take care of him, and whatever more you spend, I will repay you when I come back.' Which of these three, do you think, proved to be a neighbor to the man who fell among the robbers?" He said, "The one who showed him mercy." And Jesus said to him, "You go, and do likewise."

When you see someone in need, how do you normally respond? Why?

Why do you suppose the two religious men—the priest and the

Levite—didn't stop to help the injured man?

What can you learn from this story about God's views on how we should love people?

LOVE IS THE OVERFLOW OF JOY IN *GOD* THAT MEETS THE NEEDS OF OTHERS.

— JOHN PIPER

Think about Jesus' words to the lawyer: "You go, and do likewise." What

do those words mean to you? In what ways will you look for opportunities

to care for the needs of hurting, broken people this week?

_____

_____

_____

_____

_____

_____

_____

_____

_____

_____

_____

_____

_____

_____

A NOTE FROM CANDACE

We don't have to look far to find someone who needs something—whether it's help with finances, food and clothing, emotional support, a ride to a doctor's appointment, or a listening friend. Being the hands and feet of Jesus to those around us is one of my favorite ways to show God's love in a tangible, life-changing way.

115

Lending an Ear

PSALM 116:1–2; PROVERBS 18:2–13 (CSB)

I love the LORD because He has heard

my appeal for mercy.

Because He has turned His ear to me,

I will call out to Him as long as I live.

A fool does not delight in understanding,

but only wants to show off his opinions. . . .

The words of a person's mouth are deep waters,

a flowing river, a fountain of wisdom. . . .

A fool's lips lead to strife,

and his mouth provokes a beating.

A fool's mouth is his devastation,

and his lips are a trap for his life.

A gossip's words are like choice food

that goes down to one's innermost being. . . .

The one who gives an answer before he listens—

this is foolishness and disgrace for him.

How can listening to someone show that person you love them?

Read the first passage again. What is the psalmist's reason for loving God?

In what ways does the second passage warn us about the way we use our words and the importance of listening to people?

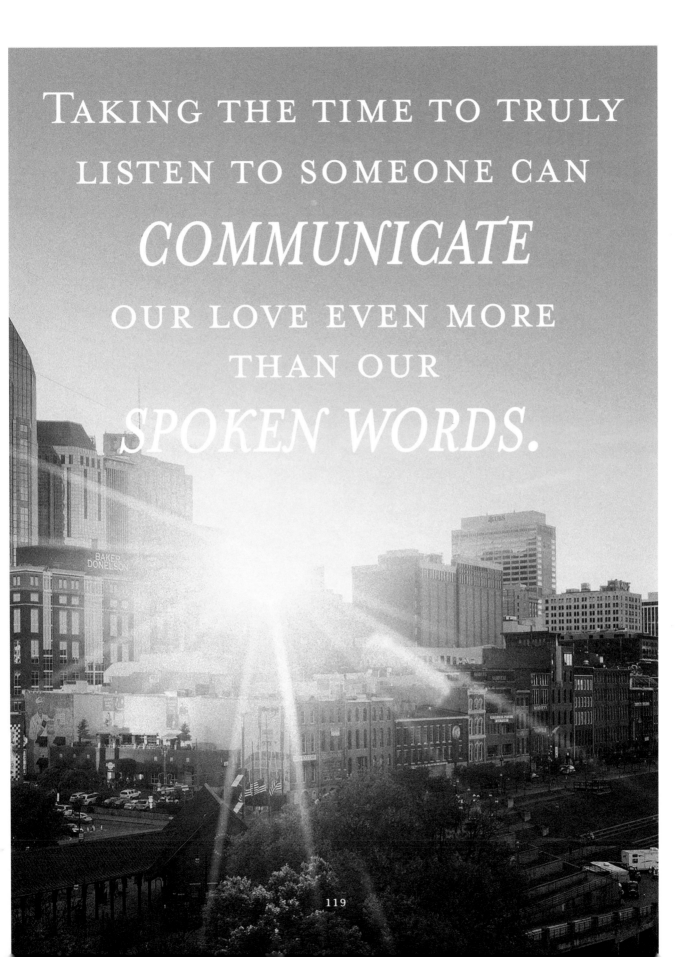

TAKING THE TIME TO TRULY LISTEN TO SOMEONE CAN *COMMUNICATE* OUR LOVE EVEN MORE THAN OUR *SPOKEN WORDS.*

Reflect on times when God answered your prayers. How did it make you

feel to know He listens and responds to you? How can you demonstrate

God's love to someone this week by being a good listener?

YOUR BIGGEST TAKEAWAY

Honoring Others

ROMANS 12:9—21 (NIV)

Love must be sincere. Hate what is evil; cling to what is good. Be devoted to one another in love. Honor one another above yourselves. Never be lacking in zeal, but keep your spiritual fervor, serving the Lord. Be joyful in hope, patient in affliction, faithful in prayer. Share with the Lord's people who are in need. Practice hospitality.

Bless those who persecute you; bless and do not curse. Rejoice with those who rejoice; mourn with those who mourn. Live in harmony with one another. Do not be proud, but be willing to associate with people of low position. Do not be conceited.

Do not repay anyone evil for evil. Be careful to do what is right in the eyes of everyone. If it is possible, as far as it depends on you, live at peace with everyone. Do not take revenge, my dear friends, but leave room for God's wrath, for it is written: "It is Mine to avenge; I will repay," says the Lord. On the contrary:

> "If your enemy is hungry, feed him;
>   if he is thirsty, give him something to drink.
> In doing this, you will heap burning coals on his head."

Do not be overcome by evil, but overcome evil with good.

What do you think it means to honor another person?

How do you honor someone who has hurt you?

In what ways are we called to love and honor people in this passage?

Based on these verses, how does God want us to treat our enemies?

HONOR ONE ANOTHER ABOVE YOURSELVES.

"Do not be overcome by evil, but overcome evil with good."

How can you put this principle into practice this week?

YOUR BIGGEST TAKEAWAY

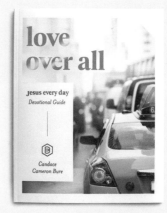